THE WEIGHT TRAINING DIARY

THE WEIGHT TRAINING DIARY

HUGO RIVERA

WILEY

John Wiley & Sons, Inc.

Published by John Wiley & Sons, Inc., Hoboken, New Jersey
Published simultaneously in Canada

Design by Forty-five Degree Design LLC

The information contained in this book is not intendd to serve as a replacement for professional medical advice. Any use of the information in this book is at the reader's discretion. The author and the publisher specifically disclaim any and all liability arising directly or indirectly from the use or application of any information contained in this book. A health care professional should be consulted regarding your specific situation.

For general information about our other products and services, please contact our Customer Care Department within the United States at (800) 762-2974, outside the United States at (317) 572-3993 or fax (317) 572-4002.

Wiley also publishes its books in a variety of electronic formats. Some content that appears in print may not be available in electronic books. For more information about Wiley products, visit our web site at www.wiley.com.

Library of Congress Cataloging-in-Publication Data:
Rivera, Hugo A., date.
  The weight training diary / by Hugo Rivera.
    p.   cm.
  ISBN 978-0-470-60740-4 (paper: alk. paper)
  1. Weight training—Handbooks, manuals, etc.   2. Bodybuilding—Handbooks, manuals, etc.   3. Diaries.   I. Title.
  GV546.R54 2010
  613.7'13—dc22

                                                                    2010028338

Printed in the United States of America
10 9 8 7 6 5 4 3 2 1

CONTENTS

INTRODUCTION

Why use a weight training diary? By recording your workouts you can see how you're progressing toward your goals, which will keep you motivated. If you're not progressing like you'd planned, your diary will help you troubleshoot your workout, which will get you back on track. And your diary will keep you accountable to that plan. Think of it as your best workout partner, an objective observer who will let you know what you need to do, keep you focused on improving, and celebrate your success with you.

I've created this diary because I've enjoyed that success myself over the past twenty years, and I know what it takes to get there. I have not only beaten the battle of the bulge by permanently losing over 70 pounds of excess weight, but also through trial and error I was able to become a successful competitive bodybuilder and best-selling fitness author.

I've helped millions of people all over the world get in shape through in-person and online training, my numerous articles on HugoRivera.net, and various online and traditional magazines such as Bodybuilding.com, DaveDraper.com, Bodybuilding.About.com, Labrada.com, *Natural Muscle*, *Olympian Muscle News*, *Maximum Fitness*, and *Physique*, just to name a few. I've also touched the lives of many people through my best-selling publications *The Body Sculpting Bible for Men*, *The Body Sculpting Bible for Women*, and *The Hardgainers' Bodybuilding Handbook*, and my online system Body Re-Engineering. With this diary I hope to help you see how you can help yourself.

Bodybuilding may sound very intimidating to many of you because it suggests overly developed muscles. In fact, bodybuilding is simply a lifestyle that incorporates weight training exercises with the proper diet, some cardiovascular exercise, and rest. Ladies, by using this diary, you will become as lean and toned as you want to be. And, gentlemen, you can become as strong and as defined as you would like to be.

If you do not want huge muscles, you do not need to worry, because they do not happen by accident. This is especially true for women, who simply do not produce the amount of testosterone needed to build an amount of muscle mass that may be considered masculine. The only way for a woman to build huge muscles like that is either by having some incredibly blessed genetics or by taking anabolic steroids or both. Obsessive-compulsive extreme training and dieting are required as well. It is not easy to grow muscles past a certain point. The more extreme your goal, the more extreme you're training, dieting, and recuperation efforts will need to be. Conversely, if all you want is to be lean and toned, you do not have to do nearly as much as you may think.

The first step, though, is getting started, and that's often the most difficult step, so I will provide you with the five key directives to incorporating weightlifting into your life—then keeping at it. I will also provide you with several sample workouts that fit a variety of goals and schedules, whether you are a beginner or a veteran, want an action hero physique, or have only thirty minutes a day to lift.

Take a look at the diary pages at the back of this book. In the first column fill in the type of set and your rest period. I discuss sets in chapter 2. Abbreviate single sets as S, modified compound supersets as MCS, supersets as SS, tri-sets as TS, and giant sets as GS.

In the second column, enter the exercise being used followed by the sets and reps you will perform. In the rest of the columns enter the amount of weight you will be using and the reps you will perform with the weight.

Below the log you will see a box labeled "Mind-Body Notes." In this box, write any thoughts on how you felt while working out, how your workout went, and so forth. In the box labeled "Nutrition Notes," write any thoughts on how you can improve your eating habits or what you are doing right with your diet. In the box labeled "Playlist" you can list the songs you listened to during the workout and how this influenced your workout in a positive or negative manner.

At the very bottom of the diary page use the boxes labeled "Cardio Activity," "Average Heart Rate," "Distance," "Start Time," and "End Time" to document the type of cardiovascular exercise used, the average heart rate during the activity, the distance traveled, and the start and end times of the activity.

The following page is an example of a filled-in diary page.

| Date 11/1/2010 | | Start Time 6:00 a.m. | | | | End Time 7:00 a.m. | |

		Set 1		Set 2		Set 3		Set 4	
Type of set (Rest ____)	Exercise (Sets ____ × Reps ____)	Weight	Reps	Weight	Reps	Weight	Reps	Weight	Reps
MCS #1 1 min	Incline DB Bench Press, 2 x 13–15	50 lbs	15	55 lbs	13				
1 min	One-Arm DB Rows, 2 x 13–15	60 lbs	15	65 lbs	13				
MCS #2 1 min	DB Bench Press, 2 x 13–15	55 lbs	15	60 lbs	13				
1 min	Pull-Down to Front, 2 x 13–15	70 lbs	15	80 lbs	13				
MCS #3 1 min	Bent-Over Lateral Raises, 2 x 13–15	30 lbs	15	35 lbs	13				
1 min	DB Shoulder Press, 2 x 13–15	40 lbs	15	45 lbs	13				
MCS #4 1 min	Incline DB Curls, 3 x 13–15	25 lbs	15	30 lbs	13	30 lbs	13		
1 min	Overhead DB Tri-Extensions, 3 x 13–15	40 lbs	15	45 lbs	13	45 lbs	13		
MCS #5 1 min	Dumbbell Lunges, 3 x 13–15	Body weight	15	20 lbs	13	20 lbs	13		
1 min	Leg Curls, 3 x 13–15	100 lbs	15	110 lbs	14	110 lbs	13		
SS #1 2 min	Squats, 3 x 13–15	150 lbs	15	160 lbs	13				
SS #2 1 min	Calf Raises, 3 x 13–15	140 lbs	15	150 lbs	13	150 lbs	13		

MIND-BODY NOTES

Woke up feeling great!

Had a lot of strength at the gym and a good pump.

Was a little tired by the end of the workout but hit the cardio with equal enthusiasm as I had with the weights.

NUTRITION NOTES

Need to make sure I get all of the water I need today.

Have to remember to take my supplements on time and not go more than 3 hours without food.

PLAYLIST

Used Techno Mix #1, which really pumped my workout up!

Cardio Activity:	Recumbent bike	
Average Heart Rate:	145 bpm	
Distance:	8 miles	
Start Time:	7:30 a.m.	End Time: 8:30 a.m.

1 THE FIVE DIRECTIVES

Before embarking on your fitness regimen, consider these five directives to help steer you toward you fitness goals. Having a clear formula will keep you focused and on track.

1. Schedule Your Commitment, Then Commit to Your Schedule

Achieving your fitness goals is both a physical and a psychological endeavor. You have to want to do it, and you have to commit the time to do it. Of course, we all get frustrated when our fitness schedules are disrupted by work, commuting, child care, household chores, and other responsibilities. So you should create a program with a time commitment that fits your schedule; then make that commitment a part of your schedule.

Some of you may not even be able to do more than three workouts a week. If this is the case, there's no issue; make the most out of the time that you do have available to train. The key to making lasting gains at the end of the day is to have a realistic plan that can be executed consistently, not to try to follow one that looks really good on paper but cannot be executed. You will get to where you want to go; it may just take a little bit longer depending on how much time you can dedicate to reaching your goals. And if you fall off the wagon, you can always get back on. The weights will still be there for you.

2. Instead of Pushing toward Your Goals, Set Goals That Pull You toward Them

Write down your long-term goals in the spaces provided on the first two pages in the diary section of this book. Break the goals down into manageable short-term goals, and give yourself realistic deadlines to achieve them. If there's a reason for the date of a goal—a wedding, a reunion, a vacation—note that too. Reaching each short-term goal will only encourage you even more to keep working hard to achieve the long-term goal that you so desire.

If you miss your goals by a bit or if they take longer to achieve than you thought they would, don't get discouraged. Consider instead the progress you have made and adjust your plan or subsequent goals accordingly. In addition to tracking your workouts in the diary, you might also take pictures of yourself before starting toward your goals and after achieving them, and clip them onto the pages. You will be able to see the difference, and that will keep you going.

If you mess up your plan for a day, don't drop the whole thing and quit. I see this very often. If you encounter one of those days, just recover the following day by picking up the plan right where you left off.

3. Visualize How You Want to Look

To motivate yourself, really try to visualize how you will look and feel once you reach your long-term goal. If you are a woman, imagine yourself in that nice dress at a party looking better than anyone else or wearing a sexy bikini. If you are a man, imagine filling out your shirts nicely, with nice pecs, a V-taper, and a tight waistline that displays a nice six-pack (not the beer kind) that you can proudly show off at any time. Imagine people admiring the way you look and asking you how they can look like that.

If you've had bad weeks where your workouts were lacking (or nonexistent) and your meals were not great, just use them as a learning experience. Whatever you could have done better, start correcting now. Most important, once you figure out what could have been improved, don't look back anymore; simply look forward and execute. No need to beat yourself up over past mistakes.

4. Train Smart

When you first get to the gym, hit a treadmill, a bike, or any piece of cardio equipment for 5 to 10 minutes at low to medium intensity. The purpose is not cardiovascular conditioning here. You are simply trying to get your body temperature up, get your blood moving into your muscles, and loosen your joints. Warming up also lowers the chance of a muscle pull or joint damage, helps you "get in the zone," makes your pumps better (as blood is already flowing into your muscles), and allows you to lift a bit more weight since your muscles will be ready.

After your warm-up cardio, focus on the specific muscles you're about to train, and build up a good pump. For your first two sets of each body part, do some light lifts to activate the muscle fibers and have them prepped for your upcoming sets. Two light sets of 15 to 20 reps will do the trick.

Whether you're warming up or working out, exercise form is important. Women are actually really good at form, but a lot of men try to max out in every single exercise, which ends up contorting them more than helping them. If you want to achieve a lean-looking physique, you must check your ego at the door.

The purpose of weight training is to target a specific muscle and stimulate it to grow. The key for success is to use a weight that allows you to put all of the resistance in the muscles and to make the intended muscles work hard. You must really focus on what you are doing as you execute the lift. If you've got poor form, you might be working the wrong muscles and end up risking injury.

If you get injured, guess what? Then you can't spend time in the gym, and you might lose the gains that you've already fought so hard to get.

Here are some guidelines for good form:

- Understand the proper execution of the movement (you can refer to my Web site www.hugorivera.net for that) and perform it through its full range of motion.
- Choose a weight that you can lift with full control. If you are not sure, choose a lighter weight.
- Focus on contracting the muscle you are working as you lift the weight.
- Don't rely on momentum or swinging, which only takes the stimulus away from the muscle and increases your chances of injury.

Whenever possible have a workout partner. A good partner can help you keep proper form, knock out your last couple of reps, and provide instant motivation throughout your workouts.

What Is the Best Repetition Range for Achieving a Defined and Toned Physique?

The routines recommended in this diary generally use a range of 6 to 15 reps (with exceptions made for body parts like calves and abs). However, I will emphasize the higher rep ranges, because by constantly challenging your muscles you continue to gain some size and increase your metabolism, which will then help you lose fat weight more quickly.

Weight selection is simple. If a particular exercise recommends you perform it for 10 to 12 reps, then when you can easily accomplish 13 reps with good form, you need to increase the poundage. If, however, you can't lift a specific weight 10 times with proper form, then drop it down a bit on the next set.

As I mentioned in the previous section, you need to choose a weight you're comfortable with and you need to pay close attention to when your muscles cannot lift it another time with good form (this point is called the point of muscular failure). If you're shooting for 12 reps and start to fail on the tenth, then you're in the right spot—fight through the last 2 reps and feel the burn as you maintain proper form (this goes for you too, ladies). If you're hitting the 12-rep range and have plenty of strength remaining, then you need to increase the plates in your next set. With time you will find the right weight for you for all lifts.

You should rest no more than ninety seconds between sets and remember to hydrate.

Cardiovascular Exercise

In order to lose body fat it is very important that you do cardio, but it is equally important that you do not overdo it. Too much cardio will start making you lose muscle mass and lower your metabolism. Fifteen to thirty-five minutes either right after a workout or first thing in the morning will suffice. Perform it at a pace that has your heart rate going between 120 to 150 beats per minute.

The benefits of cardiovascular exercise are:

- It improves cardiovascular endurance, which is critical when performing supersets.
- It helps remove waste created by the weight training session and creates new capillaries that are used to provide more nutrients to the muscle, something that helps rebuild the muscles quicker as well as recover faster in between sets and workouts.
- It prompts the body to produce fat-burning enzymes.

Any cardiovascular activity will have these effects, so just choose one that you enjoy. You can walk outside or on a treadmill. You can do the elliptical rider (my favorite), a recumbent bike, or a stair stepper.

Changing Your Workout

One of the reasons a lot of people make zero progress at the gym is their static workouts. The sample workouts I include use periodization, which is a program that varies the sets, reps, and rest periods in between sets in an orderly fashion to elicit maximum results and prevent the body from getting used to the training.

All of the workouts prescribed in this training log are twelve-week programs. After you go through any of the programs you can either:

- Create your own periodized program by following the same structure of the program you just followed but simply switching around exercises. Sets, reps, and the whole structure remain the same.
- Alternatively, if you have the time, you could progress from Workout 1 to 2 or 2 to 3, described in chapter 2.

It's entirely up to you.

When to Increase Weights

As you progress, make small changes and increase the resistance you're facing. If you've been struggling to hit 10 reps on dumbbell curls with the weight you are using but suddenly you see yourself easily doing more repetitions than prescribed, it's time to increase the weight by 5 to 10 pounds. Always remember, however, to be cautious, and if you are not too sure how much you should increase the load, just increase it by 5 pounds.

Again, when it comes to weight selection, remember that the proper weight to use is the one that will allow you to reach failure at the prescribed repetition range. If the weight you are using allows you to do more than the prescribed range, then up those weights!

If, on the other hand, the weight you are using does not allow you to perform the minimum number of the prescribed repetition range, then you need to decrease the weight so that you fall within the range.

5. Eat Right

Why isn't everyone who lifts weights sporting a nice six-pack? Most people don't achieve this because they follow the wrong nutrition program. Only when you combine the right training program with the proper nutrition will your body lose the fat and build the muscle. As I like to say, abs are built in the kitchen. For more information on proper diet and supplementation visit my Web sites www.hugorivera.net and www.bodybuilding.about.com.

2 THE WORKOUTS

Before we get to the workouts, let's review three weight training terms that you need to understand in order to perform the workouts: supersets, modified compound supersets, and giant sets.

Supersets

A superset is a set of one exercise performed right after a set of another with no rest in between; rest only between a pair of sets. You can do same-muscle supersets (e.g., dumbbell curls paired with concentration curls), but pairing antagonistic muscle groups (e.g., biceps and triceps, quads and hamstrings, front and rear delts) or muscle movements (e.g., push and pull) is more effective.

Doing supersets not only allows you to do more work in a shorter period of time, but it also increases endurance, creates an incredible pump (especially when you pair antagonistic exercises), and elevates the heart rate to the fat-burning zone (which also gives you cardiovascular benefits). And because of the stress created by this technique, growth hormone levels go through the roof; this hormone is responsible for fat loss and enhanced muscle tone.

Modified Compound Supersets

In a modified compound superset, you rest between the set of each exercise, not just between the supersets. If you rest for a minute between each set, you will thus be resting for 2 minutes plus the amount of time that it takes you to perform the other exercise (so you actually are resting a given muscle between 2.5 and 3 minutes). Using this technique not only saves time and keeps the body warm, but it also allows for faster recovery of the nervous system between sets. This will allow you to lift heavier weights than if you just stay idle for 2 to 3 minutes waiting to recover.

Giant Sets

Giant sets group sets of four or more exercises done one after the other with no rest in between the individual sets; rest only between giant sets. Like supersets, you can target either the same muscle group or perform two pairs of exercises targeting opposing muscle groups.

To target my abdominal muscles, for instance, I love to do a giant set of modified V-ups, knee-ins, bicycle crunches, and abdominal crunches, resting for a minute in between each giant set.

Doing the Workouts

Workout #1: Starter Sets

TARGET AUDIENCE

People who have never lifted weights before or those who can devote only three days a week to achieving a lean and toned physique.

TIME COMMITMENT

Three workout days, 45 to 60 minutes per workout.

TRAINING SPLIT

Full-body routine performed completely on Monday, Wednesday, and Friday, plus cardio. You can perform the ab exercises and cardio on your off days instead, preferably first thing in the morning on an empty stomach, which will provide you with a second metabolic boost. You get slightly faster results from breaking up your workout this way, and it might even fit into your schedule better.

Weeks 1 to 4

Full-Body Workout				
Type of Sets	Exercises	Sets	Repetitions	Rest
Modified Compound Supersets				
#1	Incline Dumbbell Bench Press	2	13–15	1 minute
	One-Arm Dumbbell Rows	2	13–15	1 minute
#2	Dumbbell Bench Press	2	13–15	1 minute
	Pull-Down to Front	2	13–15	1 minute
#3	Bent-Over Lateral Raises	2	13–15	1 minute
	Dumbbell Shoulder Press	2	13–15	1 minute
#4	Incline Dumbbell Curls	3	13–15	1 minute
	Overhead Dumbbell Triceps Extensions	3	13–15	1 minute
#5	Dumbbell Lunges	3	13–15	1 minute
	Leg Curls	3	13–15	1 minute
Single Sets				
#1	Squats	2	13–15	2 minutes
#2	Standing Calf Raises	3	13–15	2 minutes

Abs				
Type of Sets	Exercises	Sets	Repetitions	Rest
Modified Compound Supersets				
#1	Crunches	3	10–25	1 minute
	Leg Raises	3	10–25	1 minute

Cardio: 15 minutes

Weeks 5 to 8

Full-Body Workout				
Type of Sets	Exercises	Sets	Repetitions	Rest
Modified Compound Supersets				
#1	Incline Dumbbell Bench Press	2	10–12	1 minute
	Wide-Grip Pull-Down to Front	2	10–12	1 minute
#2	Barbell Bench Press	2	10–12	1 minute
	Close Reverse Grip Pull-Downs	2	10–12	1 minute
#3	Leg Press	3	10–12	1 minute
	Single-Legged Leg Curls	3	10–12	1 minute

(Continued)

Full-Body Workout (*Continued*)				
Type of Sets	Exercises	Sets	Repetitions	Rest
#4	Preacher Curls	3	10–12	1 minute
	Lying E-Z Triceps Extensions	3	10–12	1 minute
#5	Bent-Over Lateral Raises	3	10–12	1 minute
	Dumbbell Shoulder Press	3	10–12	1 minute
Single Sets				
#1	Lunges (Press with Toes)	2	10–12	2 minutes
#2	Standing Calf Raises	3	10–12	2 minutes

Abs				
Type of Sets	Exercises	Sets	Repetitions	Rest
Modified	Bicycle Crunches	3	10–25	1 minute
Compound	Leg Raises	3	10–25	1 minute
Supersets				
Single Set	Knee-Ins	2	10–25	1 minute

Cardio: 20 minutes

Weeks 9 to 12

Monday/Wednesday/Friday: Full-Body Workout				
Type of Sets	Exercises	Sets	Repetitions	Rest
Supersets				
#1	Incline Dumbbell Bench Press	2	8–10	0
	One-Arm Dumbbell Rows	2	8–10	90 seconds
#2	Dumbbell Bench Press	2	8–10	0
	Pull-Down to Front	2	8–10	90 seconds
#3	Bent-Over Lateral Raises	2	8–10	0
	Dumbbell Shoulder Press	2	8–10	90 seconds
#4	Incline Dumbbell Curls	3	8–10	0
	Overhead Dumbbell Triceps Extensions	3	8–10	90 seconds
#5	Dumbbell Lunges	3	8–10	0
	Leg Curls	3	8–10	90 seconds
Single Sets				
#1	Squats	3	8–10	2 minutes
#2	Standing Calf Raises	3	8–10	2 minutes

Monday/Wednesday/Friday: Abs				
Type of Sets	Exercises	Sets	Repetitions	Rest
Supersets				
#1	Knee-Ins	3	15–25	0
	Bicycle Crunches	3	15–25	90 seconds
#2	Crunches	3	15–25	0
	Leg Raises	3	15–25	90 seconds

Cardio: 25 minutes

Workout #2: The Expert

People who have been training six months or more and who can dedicate four days per week to achieving a lean and toned physique.

TIME COMMITMENT
Four workout days, 45 to 60 minutes per workout.

TRAINING SPLIT
Two-day split performed on Monday, Tuesday, Thursday, and Friday with cardio right after. You could perform the ab exercises and cardio on your off days instead, preferably first thing in the morning on an empty stomach, which will provide you with a second metabolic boost. You get slightly faster results from breaking up your workout this way, and it might even fit into your schedule better.

Weeks 1 to 4

Monday/Thursday: Chest/Back/Arms				
Type of Sets	Exercises	Sets	Repetitions	Rest
Modified Compound Supersets				
#1	Incline Dumbbell Bench Press	3	13–15	1 minute
	One-Arm Dumbbell Rows	3	13–15	1 minute
#2	Dumbbell Bench Press	2	13–15	1 minute
	V-Bar Pull-Downs	2	13–15	1 minute
#3	Dumbbell Curls	2	13–15	1 minute
	Triceps Kickbacks	2	13–15	1 minute
#4	Incline Dumbbell Curls	3	13–15	1 minute
	Overhead Dumbbell Triceps Extensions	3	13–15	1 minute

Tuesday/Friday: Shoulders/Legs/Abs				
Type of Sets	Exercises	Sets	Repetitions	Rest
Modified Compound Supersets				
#1	Bent-Over Lateral Raises	3	13–15	1 minute
	Standing Calf Raises	3	13–15	1 minute
#2	Dumbbell Shoulder Press	2	13–15	1 minute
	Seated Calf Raises	2	13–15	1 minute

(Continued)

Tuesday/Friday: Shoulders/Legs/Abs (*Continued*)				
Type of Sets	Exercises	Sets	Repetitions	Rest
#3	Dumbbell Lunges	3	13–15	1 minute
	Leg Curls	3	13–15	1 minute
#4	Leg Press	2	13–15	1 minute
	Stiff-Legged Dead Lifts	2	13–15	1 minute

All Days: Abs				
Type of Sets	Exercises	Sets	Repetitions	Rest
Modified Compound Supersets				
#1	Crunches	3	10–25	1 minute
	Leg Raises	3	10–25	1 minute
#2	Knee-Ins	3	10–25	1 minute
	Bicycle Crunches	3	10–25	1 minute

Cardio: 20 minutes

Weeks 5 to 8

Monday/Thursday: Chest/Back/Arms				
Type of Sets	Exercises	Sets	Repetitions	Rest
Supersets				
#1	Incline Dumbbell Bench Press	3	10–12	0
	One-Arm Dumbbell Rows	3	10–12	90 seconds
#2	Dumbbell Bench Press	2	10–12	0
	Pull-Down to Front	2	10–12	90 seconds
#3	Dumbbell Curls	3	10–12	0
	Triceps Kickbacks	3	10–12	90 seconds
#4	Incline Dumbbell Curls	2	10–12	0
	Overhead Dumbbell Triceps Extensions	2	10–12	90 seconds

Tuesday/Friday: Shoulders/Legs/Abs				
Type of Sets	Exercises	Sets	Repetitions	Rest
Supersets				
#1	Dumbbell Shoulder Press	3	10–12	0
	Donkey Calf Raises	3	10–12	90 seconds
#2	Rear Delt Machine	2	10–12	0
	Standing Calf Raises	2	10–12	90 seconds
#3	Squats	3	10–12	0
	Lying Leg Curls	3	10–12	90 seconds
#4	Leg Press	2	10–12	0
	Stiff-Legged Dead Lifts	2	10–12	90 seconds

All Days: Abs				
Type of Sets	Exercises	Sets	Repetitions	Rest
Supersets				
#1	Crunches	3	10–25	0
	Leg Raises	3	10–25	90 seconds
#2	Knee-Ins	3	10–25	0
	Bicycle Crunches	3	10–25	90 seconds

Cardio: 25 minutes

Weeks 9 to 12

Monday/Thursday: Chest/Back/Arms				
Type of Sets	Exercises	Sets	Repetitions	Rest
Supersets				
#1	Incline Dumbbell Bench Press	3	8–10	0
	One-Arm Dumbbell Rows	3	8–10	90 seconds
#2	Dumbbell Bench Press	3	8–10	0
	Pull-Down to Front	3	8–10	90 seconds
#3	Dumbbell Curls	3	8–10	0
	Triceps Kickbacks	3	8–10	90 seconds
#4	Incline Dumbbell Curls	3	8–10	0
	Overhead Dumbbell Triceps Extensions	3	8–10	90 seconds

Tuesday/Friday: Shoulders/Legs/Abs				
Type of Sets	Exercises	Sets	Repetitions	Rest
Supersets				
#1	Dumbbell Shoulder Press	3	8–10	0
	Donkey Calf Raises	3	8–10	90 seconds
#2	Rear Delt Machine	3	8–10	0
	Standing Calf Raises	3	8–10	90 seconds
#3	Squats	3	8–10	0
	Lying Leg Curls	3	8–10	90 seconds
#4	Leg Press	3	8–10	0
	Stiff-Legged Dead Lifts	3	8–10	90 seconds

All Days: Abs				
Type of Sets	Exercises	Sets	Repetitions	Rest
Giant Sets				
#1	Crunches	3	10–25	0
	Leg Raises	3	10–25	0
	Knee-Ins	3	10–25	0
	Bicycle Crunches	3	10–25	90 seconds

Cardio: 30 minutes

Workout #3: The Movie Star

People who have been training for a year or more and who want to achieve a very high degree of fitness by adding more muscle mass to their frames. Only those wanting to take their fitness to the level of an action-movie star or a pop star may want to try this routine.

TIME COMMITMENT

Five workout days, 45 to 60 minutes per workout.

TRAINING SPLIT

Three rotating workouts from Monday through Friday: (A) chest/back/calves; (B) shoulders/arms; and (C) legs/abs. So week 1 will end with B and week 2 will start with C before returning to A.

For these workouts, you will need to perform the cardio and the abs either right after the workout or at a separate time first thing in the morning on an empty stomach.

Weeks 1 to 4

Workout A: Chest/Back/Calves				
Type of Sets	Exercises	Sets	Repetitions	Rest
Supersets				
#1	Incline Barbell Bench Press	3	10	0
	Wide-Grip Pull-Up to Front	3	10	1 minute
#2	Dumbbell Bench Press	3	10	0
	One-Arm Dumbbell Rows	3	10	1 minute
#3	Dumbbell Flies	3	10	0
	Low Pulley Rows	3	10	1 minute
#4	Standing Calf Raises	3	10	0
	Seated Calf Raises	3	15	1 minute

Workout B: Shoulders/Arms				
Type of Sets	Exercises	Sets	Repetitions	Rest
Supersets				
#1	Bent-Over Lateral Raises	3	10	0
	Dumbbell Shoulder Press	3	10	1 minute
#2	Dumbbell Upright Rows	3	10	0
	Triceps Push-Downs	3	10	1 minute

Type of Sets	Exercises	Sets	Repetitions	Rest
#3	Dumbbell/Hammer Curls	3	10	0
	Overhead Dumbbell Triceps			
	Extensions	3	10	1 minute
#4	Preacher Curls	3	10	0
	Lying Dumbbell Triceps Extensions	3	10	1 minute

Workout C: Legs/Abs				
Type of Sets	Exercises	Sets	Repetitions	Rest
Supersets				
#1	Leg Press	3	10	0
	Lunges (Press with Heels)	3	10	1 minute
#2	Wide-Stance Squats	3	10	0
	Lying Leg Curls	3	10	1 minute
#3	Leg Extensions	3	10	0
	One-Legged Leg Curls	3	10	1 minute
#4	Crunches	3	15–25	0
	Leg Raises	3	15–25	1 minute

All Days: Abs				
Type of Sets	Exercises	Sets	Repetitions	Rest
Supersets				
#1	Leg Raises	3	10–25	0
	Ball Crunches	3	10–25	1 minute
#2	Knee-Ins	3	10–25	0
	Bicycle Crunches	3	10–25	1 minute

Cardio: 20 Minutes

Weeks 5 to 8

Continuing the cycle from weeks 1 to 4, week 5 will start with C.

Workout A: Chest/Back/Calves				
Type of Sets	Exercises	Sets	Repetitions	Rest
Modified Supersets				
#1	Incline Dumbbell Bench Press (75-degree angle on the incline)	3	10, 8, 6	90 seconds
	Neutral-Grip Pull-Ups	3	10, 8, 6	90 seconds
#2	Incline Barbell Bench Press	3	10, 8, 6	90 seconds
	Wide-Grip Pull-Up to Front	3	10, 8, 6	90 seconds
#3	Low Pulley Rows	3	10, 8, 6	90 seconds
	Incline Flies	3	10, 8, 6	90 seconds
#4	Calf Press	3	10, 8, 6	60 seconds
	Standing Calf Raises	3	10, 8, 6	60 seconds

Workout B: Shoulders/Arms				
Type of Sets	Exercises	Sets	Repetitions	Rest
Modified Supersets				
#1	Rear Delt Rows	3	10, 8, 6	90 seconds
	Military Press	3	10, 8, 6	90 seconds
#2	Barbell Upright Rows	3	10, 8, 6	90 seconds
	Triceps Push-Downs	3	10, 8, 6	90 seconds
#3	Barbell Curls	3	10, 8, 6	90 seconds
	Close-Grip Bench Press	3	10, 8, 6	90 seconds
#4	Incline Curls	3	10, 8, 6	60 seconds
	Parallel Bar Triceps Dips	3	10, 8, 6	60 seconds

Workout C: Legs/Abs				
Type of Sets	Exercises	Sets	Repetitions	Rest
Modified Supersets				
#1	Wide-Stance Squats	3	10, 8, 6	90 seconds
	Lying Leg Curls	3	10, 8, 6	90 seconds
#2	Leg Press	3	10, 8, 6	90 seconds
	Stiff-Legged Dead Lifts	3	10, 8, 6	90 seconds
#3	Barbell Lunges (Press with Ball of Foot)	3	10, 8, 6	90 seconds
	One-Legged Leg Curls	3	10, 8, 6	90 seconds
#4	Knee-Ins	3	15–25	60 seconds
	Crunches	3	15–25	60 seconds

Cardio: 35 Minutes

Weeks 9 to 12

Continuing the cycle from weeks 5 to 8, week 9 will start with B.

Workout A: Chest/Back/Calves				
Type of Sets	Exercises	Sets	Repetitions	Rest
Supersets				
#1	Incline Barbell Press	4	13–15	0
	Reverse Close-Grip Chins	4	13–15	1 minute
#2	Wide-Grip Pull-Ups to Front	3	13–15	0
	Incline Dumbbell Press	3	13–15	1 minute
#3	Chest Dips	4	13–15	0
	Low Pulley Rows	4	13–15	1 minute
#4	Calf Press	5	15–25	0
	Standing Calf Raises	5	15–25	1 minute

Workout B: Shoulders/Arms				
Type of Sets	Exercises	Sets	Repetitions	Rest
Supersets				
#1	Rear Delt Machine	4	13–15	0
	Barbell Upright Rows	4	13–15	1 minute
#2	Military Press	3	13–15	0
	Barbell Curls	3	13–15	1 minute
#3	Lying E-Z Triceps Extensions/ Close-Grip E-Z Bench Press	4	13–15	0
	Incline Curls	4	13–15	1 minute
#4	Hammer Curls Using High Pulley Rope	4	13–15	0
	Rope Push-Downs	4	13–15	1 minute

Workout C: Legs/Abs				
Type of Sets	Exercises	Sets	Repetitions	Rest
Supersets				
#1	Leg Extensions	4	13–15	0
	Leg Press	4	13–15	1 minute
#2	Stiff-Legged Dumbbell Dead Lifts	4	13–15	0
	Lunges (Press with Heels)	4	13–15	1 minute
#3	Wide-Stance Squats	3	13–15	0
	Lying Leg Curls	3	13–15	1 minute
#4	Crunches on Exercise Ball	4	15–25	0
	V-Ups	4	15–25	1 minute

All Days: Abs				
Type of Sets	Exercises	Sets	Repetitions	Rest
Giant Sets				
#1	Modified V-Ups	3	10–25	0
	Knee-Ins	3	10–25	0
	Bicycle Crunches	3	10–25	0
	Crunches	3	10–25	1 minute

Cardio: 25 minutes

Workout #4: The Lunchtime Workout

TARGET AUDIENCE

Those who can squeeze in a workout only at lunch or before or after work.

TIME COMMITMENT

Five workout days, 30 minutes per workout.

Three rotating workouts from Monday through Friday: (A) thighs/hamstrings/calves; (B) chest/back/abs; and (C) shoulders/biceps/triceps. So week 1 will end with B and week 2 will start with C before returning to A.

This workout makes up for a lack of cardio by using supersets of antagonistic muscles in order to get a cardiovascular effect.

Rest for no more than 1 minute in between supersets, tri sets, or giant sets.

Workout A: Thighs/Hamstrings/Calves			
Type of Sets	Exercises	Sets	Repetitions
Supersets			
#1	Squats	3	8–10
	Lying Leg Curls	3	8–10
#2	Leg Extensions	3	10–12
	Lunges (Pressing with Heels)	3	10–12
#3	Leg Press	3	13–15
	Seated Leg Curls	3	13–15
#4	Calf Press	3	10–12
	Standing Calf Raises	3	20–30

Workout B: Chest/Back/Abs			
Type of Sets	Exercises	Sets	Repetitions
Supersets			
#1	Incline Bench Press	3	8–10
	Wide-Grip Pull-Ups to Front	3	8–10
#2	Chest Dips	3	10–12
	Reverse Close-Grip Chins	3	10–12
#3	Incline Flies	3	13–15
	Low Pulley Rows	3	13–15
#4	Bicycle Crunches	3	10–12
	Lying Leg Raises	3	20–30

Workout C: Shoulders/Biceps/Triceps			
Type of Sets	Exercises	Sets	Repetitions
Superset	Upright Rows	3	8–10
	Military Press	3	8–10
Tri Set	Bent-Over Laterals	3	10–12
	Preacher Curls	3	8–10
	Triceps Push Downs	3	8–10
Giant Set	Hammer Curls	2	10–12
	Overhead Dumbbell Triceps Extensions	2	10–12
	Concentration Curls	2	13–15
	Lying E-Z Triceps Extensions	2	13–15

What to Do after Week 12

After week 12, assess your original goals and measure how far you have come. Did you achieve your goals? If not, then answer the following questions:

- Were your goals realistic?
- Did you follow the training plan as laid out, adhering to the recommended repetitions, exercises, and rest periods? Could you have done something better?
- Did you follow the nutrition plan? Were you skipping meals? Did you drink alcohol during the weekends?
- Did you take your nutritional supplements?
- Did you sleep at least eight hours each night?

Now that you have assessed how far you have come, be proud of your accomplishments and set new goals to get even better. Make sure that whatever component was not followed 100 percent this time around gets followed the next time for better results.

The biggest secret to long-term success from a fitness program is having the determination to stay consistent with your fitness program day in and day out for years to come, always setting new goals and achieving higher levels of development.

THE WEIGHT TRAINING DIARY

Long-Term Goals

Start date _____
Lose _____ pounds of fat
Gain _____ pounds of muscle
Weight _____ pounds

Target Measurements:
Chest _____
Arms _____
Thighs _____
Calves _____
Waist _____

Long-Term Achievements

Target end date _____
Lost _____ pounds of fat
Gained _____ pounds of muscle
Weight _____ pounds

Actual Measurements:
Chest _____
Arms _____
Thighs _____
Calves _____
Waist _____

Short-Term Goals

Start date _____
Lose _____ pounds of fat
Gain _____ pounds of muscle
Weight _____ pounds

Target Measurements:
Chest _____
Arms _____
Thighs _____
Calves _____
Waist _____

Short-Term Achievements

Target end date _____
Lost _____ pounds of fat
Gained _____ pounds of muscle
Weight _____ pounds

Actual Measurements:
Chest _____
Arms _____
Thighs _____
Calves _____
Waist _____

Short-Term Goals

Start date _____
Lose _____ pounds of fat
Gain _____ pounds of muscle
Weight _____ pounds

Target Measurements:
Chest _____
Arms _____
Thighs _____
Calves _____
Waist _____

Short-Term Achievements

Target end date _____
Lost _____ pounds of fat
Gained _____ pounds of muscle
Weight _____ pounds

Actual Measurements:
Chest _____
Arms _____
Thighs _____
Calves _____
Waist _____

Long-Term Goals

Start date _____
Lose _____ pounds of fat
Gain _____ pounds of muscle
Weight _____ pounds

Target Measurements:
Chest _____
Arms _____
Thighs _____
Calves _____
Waist _____

Long-Term Achievements

Target end date _____
Lost _____ pounds of fat
Gained _____ pounds of muscle
Weight _____ pounds

Actual Measurements:
Chest _____
Arms _____
Thighs _____
Calves _____
Waist _____

Short-Term Goals

Start date _____
Lose _____ pounds of fat
Gain _____ pounds of muscle
Weight _____ pounds

Target Measurements:
Chest _____
Arms _____
Thighs _____
Calves _____
Waist _____

Short-Term Achievements

Target end date _____
Lost _____ pounds of fat
Gained _____ pounds of muscle
Weight _____ pounds

Actual Measurements:
Chest _____
Arms _____
Thighs _____
Calves _____
Waist _____

Short-Term Goals

Start date _____
Lose _____ pounds of fat
Gain _____ pounds of muscle
Weight _____ pounds

Target Measurements:
Chest _____
Arms _____
Thighs _____
Calves _____
Waist _____

Short-Term Achievements

Target end date _____
Lost _____ pounds of fat
Gained _____ pounds of muscle
Weight _____ pounds

Actual Measurements:
Chest _____
Arms _____
Thighs _____
Calves _____
Waist _____

Date _____   Start Time _____   End Time _____

Type of set (Rest ____)	Exercise (Sets ____ × Reps ____)	Set 1 Weight	Reps	Set 2 Weight	Reps	Set 3 Weight	Reps	Set 4 Weight	Reps

MIND-BODY NOTES   **NUTRITION NOTES**   **PLAYLIST**

Cardio Activity:	
Average Heart Rate:	
Distance:	
Start Time:	End Time:

Date _____   Start Time _____   End Time _____

Type of set (Rest ____)	Exercise (Sets ____ × Reps ____)	Set 1 Weight	Reps	Set 2 Weight	Reps	Set 3 Weight	Reps	Set 4 Weight	Reps

MIND-BODY NOTES

NUTRITION NOTES

PLAYLIST

Cardio Activity:	
Average Heart Rate:	
Distance:	
Start Time:	End Time:

Date _____   Start Time _____   End Time _____

Type of set (Rest _____)	Exercise (Sets _____ × Reps _____)	Set 1 Weight	Set 1 Reps	Set 2 Weight	Set 2 Reps	Set 3 Weight	Set 3 Reps	Set 4 Weight	Set 4 Reps

MIND-BODY NOTES   **NUTRITION NOTES**   **PLAYLIST**

Cardio Activity:	
Average Heart Rate:	
Distance:	
Start Time:		End Time:	

Date _____   Start Time _____   End Time _____

Type of set (Rest ____)	Exercise (Sets ____ × Reps ____)	Set 1 Weight	Set 1 Reps	Set 2 Weight	Set 2 Reps	Set 3 Weight	Set 3 Reps	Set 4 Weight	Set 4 Reps

MIND-BODY NOTES

NUTRITION NOTES

PLAYLIST

Cardio Activity:	
Average Heart Rate:	
Distance:	
Start Time:	End Time:

Date _____ Start Time _____ End Time _____

Type of set (Rest ____)	Exercise (Sets ____ × Reps ____)	Set 1		Set 2		Set 3		Set 4	
		Weight	Reps	Weight	Reps	Weight	Reps	Weight	Reps

MIND-BODY NOTES

NUTRITION NOTES

PLAYLIST

Cardio Activity:	
Average Heart Rate:	
Distance:	
Start Time:	End Time:

Date _____ Start Time _____ End Time _____

Type of set (Rest ____)	Exercise (Sets ____ × Reps ____)	Set 1 Weight	Set 1 Reps	Set 2 Weight	Set 2 Reps	Set 3 Weight	Set 3 Reps	Set 4 Weight	Set 4 Reps

MIND-BODY NOTES

NUTRITION NOTES

PLAYLIST

Cardio Activity:	
Average Heart Rate:	
Distance:	
Start Time:		End Time:	

Date _____   Start Time _____   End Time _____

Type of set (Rest ____)	Exercise (Sets ____ × Reps ____)	Set 1		Set 2		Set 3		Set 4	
		Weight	Reps	Weight	Reps	Weight	Reps	Weight	Reps

MIND-BODY NOTES   **NUTRITION NOTES**   **PLAYLIST**

Cardio Activity:	
Average Heart Rate:	
Distance:	
Start Time:	End Time:

Date _____ Start Time _____ End Time _____

Type of set (Rest _____)	Exercise (Sets _____ × Reps _____)	Set 1		Set 2		Set 3		Set 4	
		Weight	Reps	Weight	Reps	Weight	Reps	Weight	Reps

MIND-BODY NOTES	NUTRITION NOTES	PLAYLIST

Cardio Activity:	
Average Heart Rate:	
Distance:	

Start Time:		End Time:	

Date _____   Start Time _____   End Time _____

Type of set (Rest ____)	Exercise (Sets ____ × Reps ____)	Set 1 Weight	Set 1 Reps	Set 2 Weight	Set 2 Reps	Set 3 Weight	Set 3 Reps	Set 4 Weight	Set 4 Reps

MIND-BODY NOTES   **NUTRITION NOTES**   **PLAYLIST**

Cardio Activity:	
Average Heart Rate:	
Distance:	
Start Time:	End Time:

Date _____ Start Time _____ End Time _____

Type of set (Rest ____)	Exercise (Sets ____ × Reps ____)	Set 1		Set 2		Set 3		Set 4	
		Weight	Reps	Weight	Reps	Weight	Reps	Weight	Reps

MIND-BODY NOTES	NUTRITION NOTES	PLAYLIST

Cardio Activity:	
Average Heart Rate:	
Distance:	
Start Time:	End Time:

Date _____   Start Time _____   End Time _____

Type of set (Rest ____)	Exercise (Sets ____ × Reps ____)	Set 1		Set 2		Set 3		Set 4	
		Weight	Reps	Weight	Reps	Weight	Reps	Weight	Reps

MIND-BODY NOTES   **NUTRITION NOTES**   **PLAYLIST**

Cardio Activity:	
Average Heart Rate:	
Distance:	
Start Time:	End Time:

Date _____   Start Time _____   End Time _____

Type of set (Rest ____)	Exercise (Sets ____ × Reps ____)	Set 1		Set 2		Set 3		Set 4	
		Weight	Reps	Weight	Reps	Weight	Reps	Weight	Reps

MIND-BODY NOTES   **NUTRITION NOTES**   **PLAYLIST**

Cardio Activity:	
Average Heart Rate:	
Distance:	
Start Time:	End Time:

Date _____   Start Time _____   End Time _____

Type of set (Rest ____)	Exercise (Sets ____ × Reps ____)	Set 1		Set 2		Set 3		Set 4	
		Weight	Reps	Weight	Reps	Weight	Reps	Weight	Reps

MIND-BODY NOTES

NUTRITION NOTES

PLAYLIST

Cardio Activity:	
Average Heart Rate:	
Distance:	
Start Time:	End Time:

Date _____   Start Time _____   End Time _____

Type of set (Rest ____)	Exercise (Sets ____ × Reps ____)	Set 1		Set 2		Set 3		Set 4	
		Weight	Reps	Weight	Reps	Weight	Reps	Weight	Reps

MIND-BODY NOTES

NUTRITION NOTES

PLAYLIST

Cardio Activity:	
Average Heart Rate:	
Distance:	
Start Time:		End Time:	

Date _____ Start Time _____ End Time _____

Type of set (Rest _____)	Exercise (Sets _____ × Reps _____)	Set 1		Set 2		Set 3		Set 4	
		Weight	Reps	Weight	Reps	Weight	Reps	Weight	Reps

MIND-BODY NOTES

NUTRITION NOTES

PLAYLIST

Cardio Activity:	
Average Heart Rate:	
Distance:	
Start Time:	End Time:

Date _____   Start Time _____   End Time _____

Type of set (Rest _____)	Exercise (Sets _____ × Reps _____)	Set 1		Set 2		Set 3		Set 4	
		Weight	Reps	Weight	Reps	Weight	Reps	Weight	Reps

MIND-BODY NOTES   **NUTRITION NOTES**   **PLAYLIST**

Cardio Activity:	
Average Heart Rate:	
Distance:	
Start Time:	End Time:

Date _____   Start Time _____   End Time _____

Type of set (Rest ____)	Exercise (Sets ____ × Reps ____)	Set 1		Set 2		Set 3		Set 4	
		Weight	Reps	Weight	Reps	Weight	Reps	Weight	Reps

MIND-BODY NOTES   **NUTRITION NOTES**   **PLAYLIST**

Cardio Activity:	
Average Heart Rate:	
Distance:	
Start Time:	End Time:

Date _____ Start Time _____ End Time _____

Type of set (Rest _____)	Exercise (Sets _____ × Reps _____)	Set 1		Set 2		Set 3		Set 4	
		Weight	Reps	Weight	Reps	Weight	Reps	Weight	Reps

MIND-BODY NOTES

NUTRITION NOTES

PLAYLIST

Cardio Activity:	
Average Heart Rate:	
Distance:	
Start Time:	End Time:

Date _____   Start Time _____   End Time _____

Type of set (Rest ____)	Exercise (Sets ____ × Reps ____)	Set 1		Set 2		Set 3		Set 4	
		Weight	Reps	Weight	Reps	Weight	Reps	Weight	Reps

MIND-BODY NOTES

NUTRITION NOTES

PLAYLIST

Cardio Activity:	
Average Heart Rate:	
Distance:	
Start Time:	End Time:

Date _____		Start Time _____			End Time _____				

		Set 1		Set 2		Set 3		Set 4	
Type of set (Rest ____)	Exercise (Sets ____ × Reps ____)	Weight	Reps	Weight	Reps	Weight	Reps	Weight	Reps

MIND-BODY NOTES	NUTRITION NOTES	PLAYLIST

Cardio Activity:	
Average Heart Rate:	
Distance:	

Start Time:		End Time:	

Date _____   Start Time _____   End Time _____

Type of set (Rest ____)	Exercise (Sets ____ × Reps ____)	Set 1 Weight	Reps	Set 2 Weight	Reps	Set 3 Weight	Reps	Set 4 Weight	Reps

MIND-BODY NOTES

NUTRITION NOTES

PLAYLIST

Cardio Activity:	
Average Heart Rate:	
Distance:	
Start Time:	End Time:

Date _____ Start Time _____ End Time _____

Type of set (Rest ____)	Exercise (Sets ____ × Reps ____)	Set 1 Weight	Reps	Set 2 Weight	Reps	Set 3 Weight	Reps	Set 4 Weight	Reps

MIND-BODY NOTES

NUTRITION NOTES

PLAYLIST

Cardio Activity:	
Average Heart Rate:	
Distance:	
Start Time:	End Time:

Date _____ Start Time _____ End Time _____

Type of set (Rest ____)	Exercise (Sets ____ × Reps ____)	Set 1		Set 2		Set 3		Set 4	
		Weight	Reps	Weight	Reps	Weight	Reps	Weight	Reps

MIND-BODY NOTES	NUTRITION NOTES	PLAYLIST

Cardio Activity:	
Average Heart Rate:	
Distance:	
Start Time:	End Time:

Date _____ Start Time _____ End Time _____

Type of set (Rest ____)	Exercise (Sets ____ × Reps ____)	Set 1 Weight	Set 1 Reps	Set 2 Weight	Set 2 Reps	Set 3 Weight	Set 3 Reps	Set 4 Weight	Set 4 Reps

MIND-BODY NOTES

NUTRITION NOTES

PLAYLIST

Cardio Activity:	
Average Heart Rate:	
Distance:	
Start Time:	End Time:

Date _____   Start Time _____   End Time _____

Type of set (Rest ____)	Exercise (Sets ____ × Reps ____)	Set 1		Set 2		Set 3		Set 4	
		Weight	Reps	Weight	Reps	Weight	Reps	Weight	Reps

MIND-BODY NOTES	NUTRITION NOTES	PLAYLIST

Cardio Activity:	
Average Heart Rate:	
Distance:	

Start Time:		End Time:	

Date _____ Start Time _____ End Time _____

Type of set (Rest _____)	Exercise (Sets _____ × Reps _____)	Set 1		Set 2		Set 3		Set 4	
		Weight	Reps	Weight	Reps	Weight	Reps	Weight	Reps

MIND-BODY NOTES	NUTRITION NOTES	PLAYLIST

Cardio Activity:	
Average Heart Rate:	
Distance:	
Start Time:	End Time:

Date _____   Start Time _____   End Time _____

Type of set (Rest _____)	Exercise (Sets _____ × Reps _____)	Set 1		Set 2		Set 3		Set 4	
		Weight	Reps	Weight	Reps	Weight	Reps	Weight	Reps

MIND-BODY NOTES

NUTRITION NOTES

PLAYLIST

Cardio Activity:	
Average Heart Rate:	
Distance:	
Start Time:	End Time:

Date _____ Start Time _____ End Time _____

Type of set (Rest _____)	Exercise (Sets _____ × Reps _____)	Set 1		Set 2		Set 3		Set 4	
		Weight	Reps	Weight	Reps	Weight	Reps	Weight	Reps

MIND-BODY NOTES

NUTRITION NOTES

PLAYLIST

Cardio Activity:	
Average Heart Rate:	
Distance:	
Start Time:	End Time:

Date _____   Start Time _____   End Time _____

Type of set (Rest _____)	Exercise (Sets _____ × Reps _____)	Set 1		Set 2		Set 3		Set 4	
		Weight	Reps	Weight	Reps	Weight	Reps	Weight	Reps

MIND-BODY NOTES

NUTRITION NOTES

PLAYLIST

Cardio Activity:	
Average Heart Rate:	
Distance:	
Start Time:	End Time:

Date _____   Start Time _____   End Time _____

Type of set (Rest _____)	Exercise (Sets _____ × Reps _____)	Set 1		Set 2		Set 3		Set 4	
		Weight	Reps	Weight	Reps	Weight	Reps	Weight	Reps

MIND-BODY NOTES	NUTRITION NOTES	PLAYLIST

Cardio Activity:	
Average Heart Rate:	
Distance:	

Start Time:		End Time:	

Date _____   Start Time _____   End Time _____

Type of set (Rest ____)	Exercise (Sets ____ × Reps ____)	Set 1 Weight	Reps	Set 2 Weight	Reps	Set 3 Weight	Reps	Set 4 Weight	Reps

MIND-BODY NOTES   **NUTRITION NOTES**   **PLAYLIST**

Cardio Activity:	
Average Heart Rate:	
Distance:	
Start Time:	End Time:

Date _____   Start Time _____   End Time _____

Type of set (Rest _____)	Exercise (Sets _____ × Reps _____)	Set 1		Set 2		Set 3		Set 4	
		Weight	Reps	Weight	Reps	Weight	Reps	Weight	Reps

MIND-BODY NOTES   **NUTRITION NOTES**   **PLAYLIST**

Cardio Activity:	
Average Heart Rate:	
Distance:	
Start Time:	End Time:

Date _____   Start Time _____   End Time _____

Type of set (Rest ____)	Exercise (Sets ____ × Reps ____)	Set 1 Weight	Reps	Set 2 Weight	Reps	Set 3 Weight	Reps	Set 4 Weight	Reps

MIND-BODY NOTES   **NUTRITION NOTES**   **PLAYLIST**

Cardio Activity:	
Average Heart Rate:	
Distance:	
Start Time:	End Time:

Date _____ Start Time _____ End Time _____

Type of set (Rest ____)	Exercise (Sets ____ × Reps ____)	Set 1		Set 2		Set 3		Set 4	
		Weight	Reps	Weight	Reps	Weight	Reps	Weight	Reps

MIND-BODY NOTES	NUTRITION NOTES	PLAYLIST

Cardio Activity:	
Average Heart Rate:	
Distance:	

Start Time:		End Time:	

Date _____   Start Time _____   End Time _____

Type of set (Rest ____)	Exercise (Sets ____ × Reps ____)	Set 1 Weight	Reps	Set 2 Weight	Reps	Set 3 Weight	Reps	Set 4 Weight	Reps

MIND-BODY NOTES

NUTRITION NOTES

PLAYLIST

Cardio Activity:	
Average Heart Rate:	
Distance:	
Start Time:	End Time:

Date _____ Start Time _____ End Time _____

Type of set (Rest ____)	Exercise (Sets ____ × Reps ____)	Set 1		Set 2		Set 3		Set 4	
		Weight	Reps	Weight	Reps	Weight	Reps	Weight	Reps

MIND-BODY NOTES	NUTRITION NOTES	PLAYLIST

Cardio Activity:	
Average Heart Rate:	
Distance:	

Start Time:		End Time:	

Date _____ Start Time _____ End Time _____

Type of set (Rest ____)	Exercise (Sets ____ × Reps ____)	Set 1		Set 2		Set 3		Set 4	
		Weight	Reps	Weight	Reps	Weight	Reps	Weight	Reps

MIND-BODY NOTES

NUTRITION NOTES

PLAYLIST

Cardio Activity:	
Average Heart Rate:	
Distance:	
Start Time:	End Time:

Date _____ Start Time _____ End Time _____

Type of set (Rest ___)	Exercise (Sets ___ × Reps ___)	Set 1		Set 2		Set 3		Set 4	
		Weight	Reps	Weight	Reps	Weight	Reps	Weight	Reps

MIND-BODY NOTES

NUTRITION NOTES

PLAYLIST

Cardio Activity:	
Average Heart Rate:	
Distance:	
Start Time:	End Time:

Date _____   Start Time _____   End Time _____

Type of set (Rest ____)	Exercise (Sets ____ × Reps ____)	Set 1		Set 2		Set 3		Set 4	
		Weight	Reps	Weight	Reps	Weight	Reps	Weight	Reps

MIND-BODY NOTES	NUTRITION NOTES	PLAYLIST

Cardio Activity:	
Average Heart Rate:	
Distance:	
Start Time:	End Time:

| Date _____ | Start Time _____ | End Time _____ |

Type of set (Rest ____)	Exercise (Sets ____ × Reps ____)	Set 1		Set 2		Set 3		Set 4	
		Weight	Reps	Weight	Reps	Weight	Reps	Weight	Reps

MIND-BODY NOTES

NUTRITION NOTES

PLAYLIST

Cardio Activity:	
Average Heart Rate:	
Distance:	
Start Time:	End Time:

Date _____ Start Time _____ End Time _____

Type of set (Rest ____)	Exercise (Sets ____ × Reps ____)	Set 1		Set 2		Set 3		Set 4	
		Weight	Reps	Weight	Reps	Weight	Reps	Weight	Reps

MIND-BODY NOTES	NUTRITION NOTES	PLAYLIST

Cardio Activity:	
Average Heart Rate:	
Distance:	
Start Time:	End Time:

Date _____		Start Time _____		End Time _____					
		Set 1		**Set 2**		**Set 3**		**Set 4**	
Type of set (Rest ____)	Exercise (Sets ____ × Reps ____)	Weight	Reps	Weight	Reps	Weight	Reps	Weight	Reps

MIND-BODY NOTES	NUTRITION NOTES	PLAYLIST

Cardio Activity:	
Average Heart Rate:	
Distance:	
Start Time:	End Time:

Date _____   Start Time _____   End Time _____

Type of set (Rest _____)	Exercise (Sets _____ × Reps _____)	Set 1		Set 2		Set 3		Set 4	
		Weight	Reps	Weight	Reps	Weight	Reps	Weight	Reps

MIND-BODY NOTES	NUTRITION NOTES	PLAYLIST

Cardio Activity:	
Average Heart Rate:	
Distance:	
Start Time:	End Time:

Date _____   Start Time _____   End Time _____

Type of set (Rest ____)	Exercise (Sets ____ × Reps ____)	Set 1 Weight	Reps	Set 2 Weight	Reps	Set 3 Weight	Reps	Set 4 Weight	Reps

MIND-BODY NOTES	NUTRITION NOTES	PLAYLIST

Cardio Activity:	
Average Heart Rate:	
Distance:	
Start Time:	End Time:

Date _____   Start Time _____   End Time _____

Type of set (Rest _____)	Exercise (Sets _____ × Reps _____)	Set 1		Set 2		Set 3		Set 4	
		Weight	Reps	Weight	Reps	Weight	Reps	Weight	Reps

MIND-BODY NOTES	NUTRITION NOTES	PLAYLIST

Cardio Activity:	
Average Heart Rate:	
Distance:	
Start Time:	End Time:

Date _____ Start Time _____ End Time _____

Type of set (Rest _____)	Exercise (Sets _____ × Reps _____)	Set 1 Weight	Reps	Set 2 Weight	Reps	Set 3 Weight	Reps	Set 4 Weight	Reps

MIND-BODY NOTES

NUTRITION NOTES

PLAYLIST

Cardio Activity:	
Average Heart Rate:	
Distance:	
Start Time:	End Time:

Date _____   Start Time _____   End Time _____

Type of set (Rest ____)	Exercise (Sets ____ × Reps ____)	Set 1 Weight	Set 1 Reps	Set 2 Weight	Set 2 Reps	Set 3 Weight	Set 3 Reps	Set 4 Weight	Set 4 Reps

MIND-BODY NOTES	NUTRITION NOTES	PLAYLIST

Cardio Activity:	
Average Heart Rate:	
Distance:	
Start Time:	End Time:

Date _____ Start Time _____ End Time _____

Type of set (Rest ____)	Exercise (Sets ____ × Reps ____)	Set 1		Set 2		Set 3		Set 4	
		Weight	Reps	Weight	Reps	Weight	Reps	Weight	Reps

MIND-BODY NOTES   **NUTRITION NOTES**   **PLAYLIST**

Cardio Activity:	
Average Heart Rate:	
Distance:	
Start Time:	End Time:

Date _____   Start Time _____   End Time _____

Type of set (Rest ____)	Exercise (Sets ____ × Reps ____)	Set 1 Weight	Set 1 Reps	Set 2 Weight	Set 2 Reps	Set 3 Weight	Set 3 Reps	Set 4 Weight	Set 4 Reps

MIND-BODY NOTES

NUTRITION NOTES

PLAYLIST

Cardio Activity:	
Average Heart Rate:	
Distance:	
Start Time:	End Time:

Date _____ Start Time _____ End Time _____

Type of set (Rest ____)	Exercise (Sets ____ × Reps ____)	Set 1		Set 2		Set 3		Set 4	
		Weight	Reps	Weight	Reps	Weight	Reps	Weight	Reps

MIND-BODY NOTES

NUTRITION NOTES

PLAYLIST

Cardio Activity:	
Average Heart Rate:	
Distance:	
Start Time:	End Time:

Date _____   Start Time _____   End Time _____

Type of set (Rest ____)	Exercise (Sets ____ × Reps ____)	Set 1		Set 2		Set 3		Set 4	
		Weight	Reps	Weight	Reps	Weight	Reps	Weight	Reps

MIND-BODY NOTES	NUTRITION NOTES	PLAYLIST

Cardio Activity:	
Average Heart Rate:	
Distance:	
Start Time:	End Time:

Date _____   Start Time _____   End Time _____

Type of set (Rest ____)	Exercise (Sets ____ × Reps ____)	Set 1		Set 2		Set 3		Set 4	
		Weight	Reps	Weight	Reps	Weight	Reps	Weight	Reps

MIND-BODY NOTES	NUTRITION NOTES	PLAYLIST

Cardio Activity:	
Average Heart Rate:	
Distance:	
Start Time:	End Time:

Date _____ Start Time _____ End Time _____

Type of set (Rest ___)	Exercise (Sets ___ × Reps ___)	Set 1		Set 2		Set 3		Set 4	
		Weight	Reps	Weight	Reps	Weight	Reps	Weight	Reps

MIND-BODY NOTES	NUTRITION NOTES	PLAYLIST

Cardio Activity:	
Average Heart Rate:	
Distance:	
Start Time:	End Time:

Date _____ Start Time _____ End Time _____

Type of set (Rest ____)	Exercise (Sets ____ × Reps ____)	Set 1		Set 2		Set 3		Set 4	
		Weight	Reps	Weight	Reps	Weight	Reps	Weight	Reps

MIND-BODY NOTES	NUTRITION NOTES	PLAYLIST

Cardio Activity:	
Average Heart Rate:	
Distance:	
Start Time:	End Time:

Date _____   Start Time _____   End Time _____

Type of set (Rest ____)	Exercise (Sets ____ × Reps ____)	Set 1 Weight	Reps	Set 2 Weight	Reps	Set 3 Weight	Reps	Set 4 Weight	Reps

MIND-BODY NOTES	NUTRITION NOTES	PLAYLIST

Cardio Activity:	
Average Heart Rate:	
Distance:	
Start Time:	End Time:

Date _____ Start Time _____ End Time _____

Type of set (Rest ____)	Exercise (Sets ____ × Reps ____)	Set 1		Set 2		Set 3		Set 4	
		Weight	Reps	Weight	Reps	Weight	Reps	Weight	Reps

MIND-BODY NOTES	NUTRITION NOTES	PLAYLIST

Cardio Activity:	
Average Heart Rate:	
Distance:	

Start Time:		End Time:	

Date _____ Start Time _____ End Time _____

Type of set (Rest _____)	Exercise (Sets _____ × Reps _____)	Set 1		Set 2		Set 3		Set 4	
		Weight	Reps	Weight	Reps	Weight	Reps	Weight	Reps

MIND-BODY NOTES	NUTRITION NOTES	PLAYLIST

Cardio Activity:	
Average Heart Rate:	
Distance:	

Start Time:		End Time:	

Date _____ Start Time _____ End Time _____

Type of set (Rest _____)	Exercise (Sets _____ × Reps _____)	Set 1		Set 2		Set 3		Set 4	
		Weight	Reps	Weight	Reps	Weight	Reps	Weight	Reps

MIND-BODY NOTES	NUTRITION NOTES	PLAYLIST

Cardio Activity:	
Average Heart Rate:	
Distance:	
Start Time:	End Time:

Date _____ Start Time _____ End Time _____

Type of set (Rest _____)	Exercise (Sets _____ × Reps _____)	Set 1		Set 2		Set 3		Set 4	
		Weight	Reps	Weight	Reps	Weight	Reps	Weight	Reps

MIND-BODY NOTES	NUTRITION NOTES	PLAYLIST

Cardio Activity:	
Average Heart Rate:	
Distance:	
Start Time:	End Time:

Date _____   Start Time _____   End Time _____

Type of set (Rest ____)	Exercise (Sets ____ × Reps ____)	Set 1		Set 2		Set 3		Set 4	
		Weight	Reps	Weight	Reps	Weight	Reps	Weight	Reps

MIND-BODY NOTES	NUTRITION NOTES	PLAYLIST

Cardio Activity:	
Average Heart Rate:	
Distance:	

Start Time:		End Time:	

Date _____   Start Time _____   End Time _____

Type of set (Rest ____)	Exercise (Sets ____ × Reps ____)	Set 1		Set 2		Set 3		Set 4	
		Weight	Reps	Weight	Reps	Weight	Reps	Weight	Reps

MIND-BODY NOTES

NUTRITION NOTES

PLAYLIST

Cardio Activity:	
Average Heart Rate:	
Distance:	
Start Time:	End Time:

Date _____ Start Time _____ End Time _____

Type of set (Rest _____)	Exercise (Sets _____ × Reps _____)	Set 1		Set 2		Set 3		Set 4	
		Weight	Reps	Weight	Reps	Weight	Reps	Weight	Reps

MIND-BODY NOTES   **NUTRITION NOTES**   **PLAYLIST**

Cardio Activity:	
Average Heart Rate:	
Distance:	
Start Time:	End Time:

Date _____   Start Time _____   End Time _____

Type of set (Rest _____)	Exercise (Sets _____ × Reps _____)	Set 1		Set 2		Set 3		Set 4	
		Weight	Reps	Weight	Reps	Weight	Reps	Weight	Reps

MIND-BODY NOTES	NUTRITION NOTES	PLAYLIST

Cardio Activity:	
Average Heart Rate:	
Distance:	
Start Time:	End Time:

Date _____   Start Time _____   End Time _____

Type of set (Rest ____)	Exercise (Sets ____ × Reps ____)	Set 1		Set 2		Set 3		Set 4	
		Weight	Reps	Weight	Reps	Weight	Reps	Weight	Reps

MIND-BODY NOTES

NUTRITION NOTES

PLAYLIST

Cardio Activity:	
Average Heart Rate:	
Distance:	
Start Time:	End Time:

Date _____   Start Time _____   End Time _____

Type of set (Rest ____)	Exercise (Sets ____ × Reps ____)	Set 1		Set 2		Set 3		Set 4	
		Weight	Reps	Weight	Reps	Weight	Reps	Weight	Reps

MIND-BODY NOTES	NUTRITION NOTES	PLAYLIST

Cardio Activity:	
Average Heart Rate:	
Distance:	
Start Time:	End Time:

Date _____   Start Time _____   End Time _____

Type of set (Rest ____)	Exercise (Sets ____ × Reps ____)	Set 1		Set 2		Set 3		Set 4	
		Weight	Reps	Weight	Reps	Weight	Reps	Weight	Reps

MIND-BODY NOTES

NUTRITION NOTES

PLAYLIST

Cardio Activity:	
Average Heart Rate:	
Distance:	
Start Time:		End Time:	

Date _____ Start Time _____ End Time _____

Type of set (Rest ____)	Exercise (Sets ____ × Reps ____)	Set 1		Set 2		Set 3		Set 4	
		Weight	Reps	Weight	Reps	Weight	Reps	Weight	Reps

MIND-BODY NOTES	NUTRITION NOTES	PLAYLIST

Cardio Activity:	
Average Heart Rate:	
Distance:	
Start Time:	End Time:

Date _____ Start Time _____ End Time _____

Type of set (Rest ____)	Exercise (Sets ____ × Reps ____)	Set 1		Set 2		Set 3		Set 4	
		Weight	Reps	Weight	Reps	Weight	Reps	Weight	Reps

MIND-BODY NOTES	NUTRITION NOTES	PLAYLIST

Cardio Activity:	
Average Heart Rate:	
Distance:	
Start Time:	End Time:

Date _____   Start Time _____   End Time _____

Type of set (Rest ____)	Exercise (Sets ____ × Reps ____)	Set 1 Weight	Reps	Set 2 Weight	Reps	Set 3 Weight	Reps	Set 4 Weight	Reps

MIND-BODY NOTES

NUTRITION NOTES

PLAYLIST

Cardio Activity:	
Average Heart Rate:	
Distance:	
Start Time:	End Time:

Date _____   Start Time _____   End Time _____

Type of set (Rest ____)	Exercise (Sets ____ × Reps ____)	Set 1 Weight	Reps	Set 2 Weight	Reps	Set 3 Weight	Reps	Set 4 Weight	Reps

MIND-BODY NOTES   NUTRITION NOTES   PLAYLIST

Cardio Activity:	
Average Heart Rate:	
Distance:	
Start Time:	End Time:

Date _____   Start Time _____   End Time _____

Type of set (Rest _____)	Exercise (Sets _____ × Reps _____)	Set 1		Set 2		Set 3		Set 4	
		Weight	Reps	Weight	Reps	Weight	Reps	Weight	Reps

MIND-BODY NOTES	NUTRITION NOTES	PLAYLIST

Cardio Activity:	
Average Heart Rate:	
Distance:	

Start Time:		End Time:	

Date _____ Start Time _____ End Time _____

Type of set (Rest _____)	Exercise (Sets _____ × Reps _____)	Set 1		Set 2		Set 3		Set 4	
		Weight	Reps	Weight	Reps	Weight	Reps	Weight	Reps

MIND-BODY NOTES

NUTRITION NOTES

PLAYLIST

Cardio Activity:	
Average Heart Rate:	
Distance:	
Start Time:	End Time:

Date _____   Start Time _____   End Time _____

Type of set (Rest _____)	Exercise (Sets _____ × Reps _____)	Set 1		Set 2		Set 3		Set 4	
		Weight	Reps	Weight	Reps	Weight	Reps	Weight	Reps

MIND-BODY NOTES

NUTRITION NOTES

PLAYLIST

Cardio Activity:	
Average Heart Rate:	
Distance:	
Start Time:	End Time:

Date _____ Start Time _____ End Time _____

Type of set (Rest ____)	Exercise (Sets ____ × Reps ____)	Set 1		Set 2		Set 3		Set 4	
		Weight	Reps	Weight	Reps	Weight	Reps	Weight	Reps

MIND-BODY NOTES

NUTRITION NOTES

PLAYLIST

Cardio Activity:	
Average Heart Rate:	
Distance:	
Start Time:	End Time:

Date _____ Start Time _____ End Time _____

Type of set (Rest ____)	Exercise (Sets ____ × Reps ____)	Set 1		Set 2		Set 3		Set 4	
		Weight	Reps	Weight	Reps	Weight	Reps	Weight	Reps

MIND-BODY NOTES **NUTRITION NOTES** **PLAYLIST**

Cardio Activity:	
Average Heart Rate:	
Distance:	
Start Time:		End Time:	

Date _____		Start Time _____		End Time _____				

		Set 1		Set 2		Set 3		Set 4	
Type of set (Rest _____)	Exercise (Sets _____ × Reps _____)	Weight	Reps	Weight	Reps	Weight	Reps	Weight	Reps

MIND-BODY NOTES	NUTRITION NOTES	PLAYLIST

Cardio Activity:	
Average Heart Rate:	
Distance:	
Start Time:	End Time:

Date _____ Start Time _____ End Time _____

Type of set (Rest _____)	Exercise (Sets _____ × Reps _____)	Set 1		Set 2		Set 3		Set 4	
		Weight	Reps	Weight	Reps	Weight	Reps	Weight	Reps

MIND-BODY NOTES	NUTRITION NOTES	PLAYLIST

Cardio Activity:	
Average Heart Rate:	
Distance:	
Start Time:	End Time:

Date _____ Start Time _____ End Time _____

Type of set (Rest ____)	Exercise (Sets ____ × Reps ____)	Set 1		Set 2		Set 3		Set 4	
		Weight	Reps	Weight	Reps	Weight	Reps	Weight	Reps

MIND-BODY NOTES	NUTRITION NOTES	PLAYLIST

Cardio Activity:	
Average Heart Rate:	
Distance:	
Start Time:	End Time:

Date _____   Start Time _____   End Time _____

Type of set (Rest ____)	Exercise (Sets ____ × Reps ____)	Set 1		Set 2		Set 3		Set 4	
		Weight	Reps	Weight	Reps	Weight	Reps	Weight	Reps

MIND-BODY NOTES

NUTRITION NOTES

PLAYLIST

Cardio Activity:	
Average Heart Rate:	
Distance:	
Start Time:	End Time:

Date _____ Start Time _____ End Time _____

Type of set (Rest ____)	Exercise (Sets ____ × Reps ____)	Set 1		Set 2		Set 3		Set 4	
		Weight	Reps	Weight	Reps	Weight	Reps	Weight	Reps

MIND-BODY NOTES   NUTRITION NOTES   PLAYLIST

Cardio Activity:	
Average Heart Rate:	
Distance:	
Start Time:	End Time:

Date _____ Start Time _____ End Time _____

Type of set (Rest ____)	Exercise (Sets ____ × Reps ____)	Set 1 Weight	Reps	Set 2 Weight	Reps	Set 3 Weight	Reps	Set 4 Weight	Reps

MIND-BODY NOTES	NUTRITION NOTES	PLAYLIST

Cardio Activity:	
Average Heart Rate:	
Distance:	
Start Time:	End Time:

Date _____   Start Time _____   End Time _____

Type of set (Rest ____)	Exercise (Sets ____ × Reps ____)	Set 1		Set 2		Set 3		Set 4	
		Weight	Reps	Weight	Reps	Weight	Reps	Weight	Reps

MIND-BODY NOTES   **NUTRITION NOTES**   **PLAYLIST**

Cardio Activity:	
Average Heart Rate:	
Distance:	
Start Time:	End Time:

Date _____ Start Time _____ End Time _____

Type of set (Rest ____)	Exercise (Sets ____ × Reps ____)	Set 1		Set 2		Set 3		Set 4	
		Weight	Reps	Weight	Reps	Weight	Reps	Weight	Reps

MIND-BODY NOTES

NUTRITION NOTES

PLAYLIST

Cardio Activity:	
Average Heart Rate:	
Distance:	
Start Time:	End Time:

Date _____ Start Time _____ End Time _____

Type of set (Rest _____)	Exercise (Sets _____ × Reps _____)	Set 1		Set 2		Set 3		Set 4	
		Weight	Reps	Weight	Reps	Weight	Reps	Weight	Reps

MIND-BODY NOTES   **NUTRITION NOTES**   **PLAYLIST**

Cardio Activity:	
Average Heart Rate:	
Distance:	
Start Time:	End Time:

Date _____   Start Time _____   End Time _____

Type of set (Rest ____)	Exercise (Sets ____ × Reps ____)	Set 1 Weight	Reps	Set 2 Weight	Reps	Set 3 Weight	Reps	Set 4 Weight	Reps

MIND-BODY NOTES	NUTRITION NOTES	PLAYLIST

Cardio Activity:	
Average Heart Rate:	
Distance:	
Start Time:		End Time:	

Date _____ Start Time _____ End Time _____

Type of set (Rest _____)	Exercise (Sets _____ × Reps _____)	Set 1		Set 2		Set 3		Set 4	
		Weight	Reps	Weight	Reps	Weight	Reps	Weight	Reps

MIND-BODY NOTES	NUTRITION NOTES	PLAYLIST

Cardio Activity:	
Average Heart Rate:	
Distance:	

Start Time:		End Time:	

Date _____   Start Time _____   End Time _____

Type of set (Rest _____)	Exercise (Sets _____ × Reps _____)	Set 1		Set 2		Set 3		Set 4	
		Weight	Reps	Weight	Reps	Weight	Reps	Weight	Reps

MIND-BODY NOTES

NUTRITION NOTES

PLAYLIST

Cardio Activity:	
Average Heart Rate:	
Distance:	
Start Time:	End Time:

Date _____   Start Time _____   End Time _____

Type of set (Rest ____)	Exercise (Sets ____ × Reps ____)	Set 1 Weight	Reps	Set 2 Weight	Reps	Set 3 Weight	Reps	Set 4 Weight	Reps

MIND-BODY NOTES	NUTRITION NOTES	PLAYLIST

Cardio Activity:	
Average Heart Rate:	
Distance:	
Start Time:	End Time:

Date _____ Start Time _____ End Time _____

Type of set (Rest _____)	Exercise (Sets _____ × Reps _____)	Set 1		Set 2		Set 3		Set 4	
		Weight	Reps	Weight	Reps	Weight	Reps	Weight	Reps

MIND-BODY NOTES	NUTRITION NOTES	PLAYLIST

Cardio Activity:	
Average Heart Rate:	
Distance:	

Start Time:		End Time:	

Date _____   Start Time _____   End Time _____

Type of set (Rest ____)	Exercise (Sets ____ × Reps ____)	Set 1		Set 2		Set 3		Set 4	
		Weight	Reps	Weight	Reps	Weight	Reps	Weight	Reps

MIND-BODY NOTES	NUTRITION NOTES	PLAYLIST

Cardio Activity:	
Average Heart Rate:	
Distance:	
Start Time:	End Time:

Date _____ Start Time _____ End Time _____

Type of set (Rest _____)	Exercise (Sets _____ × Reps _____)	Set 1		Set 2		Set 3		Set 4	
		Weight	Reps	Weight	Reps	Weight	Reps	Weight	Reps

MIND-BODY NOTES	NUTRITION NOTES	PLAYLIST

Cardio Activity:	
Average Heart Rate:	
Distance:	
Start Time:	End Time:

Date _____   Start Time _____   End Time _____

Type of set (Rest ____)	Exercise (Sets ____ × Reps ____)	Set 1 Weight	Set 1 Reps	Set 2 Weight	Set 2 Reps	Set 3 Weight	Set 3 Reps	Set 4 Weight	Set 4 Reps

MIND-BODY NOTES

NUTRITION NOTES

PLAYLIST

Cardio Activity:	
Average Heart Rate:	
Distance:	
Start Time:	End Time:

Date _____   Start Time _____   End Time _____

Type of set (Rest ____)	Exercise (Sets ____ × Reps ____)	Set 1		Set 2		Set 3		Set 4	
		Weight	Reps	Weight	Reps	Weight	Reps	Weight	Reps

MIND-BODY NOTES	NUTRITION NOTES	PLAYLIST

Cardio Activity:	
Average Heart Rate:	
Distance:	
Start Time:	End Time:

Date _____ Start Time _____ End Time _____

Type of set (Rest ____)	Exercise (Sets ____ × Reps ____)	Set 1		Set 2		Set 3		Set 4	
		Weight	Reps	Weight	Reps	Weight	Reps	Weight	Reps

MIND-BODY NOTES   **NUTRITION NOTES**   **PLAYLIST**

Cardio Activity:	
Average Heart Rate:	
Distance:	
Start Time:	End Time:

Date _____   Start Time _____   End Time _____

Type of set (Rest ____)	Exercise (Sets ____ × Reps ____)	Set 1		Set 2		Set 3		Set 4	
		Weight	Reps	Weight	Reps	Weight	Reps	Weight	Reps

MIND-BODY NOTES

NUTRITION NOTES

PLAYLIST

Cardio Activity:	
Average Heart Rate:	
Distance:	
Start Time:	End Time:

Date _____ Start Time _____ End Time _____

Type of set (Rest ____)	Exercise (Sets ____ × Reps ____)	Set 1		Set 2		Set 3		Set 4	
		Weight	Reps	Weight	Reps	Weight	Reps	Weight	Reps

MIND-BODY NOTES	NUTRITION NOTES	PLAYLIST

Cardio Activity:	
Average Heart Rate:	
Distance:	

Start Time:		End Time:	

Date _____   Start Time _____   End Time _____

Type of set (Rest ____)	Exercise (Sets ____ × Reps ____)	Set 1		Set 2		Set 3		Set 4	
		Weight	Reps	Weight	Reps	Weight	Reps	Weight	Reps

MIND-BODY NOTES	NUTRITION NOTES	PLAYLIST

Cardio Activity:	
Average Heart Rate:	
Distance:	

Start Time:		End Time:	

Date _____   Start Time _____   End Time _____

Type of set (Rest ____)	Exercise (Sets ____ × Reps ____)	Set 1		Set 2		Set 3		Set 4	
		Weight	Reps	Weight	Reps	Weight	Reps	Weight	Reps

MIND-BODY NOTES	NUTRITION NOTES	PLAYLIST

Cardio Activity:	
Average Heart Rate:	
Distance:	
Start Time:	End Time:

Date _____ Start Time _____ End Time _____

Type of set (Rest ___)	Exercise (Sets ___ × Reps ___)	Set 1		Set 2		Set 3		Set 4	
		Weight	Reps	Weight	Reps	Weight	Reps	Weight	Reps

MIND-BODY NOTES

NUTRITION NOTES

PLAYLIST

Cardio Activity:	
Average Heart Rate:	
Distance:	
Start Time:	End Time:

Date _____ Start Time _____ End Time _____

Type of set (Rest ____)	Exercise (Sets ____ × Reps ____)	Set 1		Set 2		Set 3		Set 4	
		Weight	Reps	Weight	Reps	Weight	Reps	Weight	Reps

MIND-BODY NOTES	NUTRITION NOTES	PLAYLIST

Cardio Activity:	
Average Heart Rate:	
Distance:	

Start Time:		End Time:	

Date _____ Start Time _____ End Time _____

Type of set (Rest ____)	Exercise (Sets ____ × Reps ____)	Set 1 Weight	Reps	Set 2 Weight	Reps	Set 3 Weight	Reps	Set 4 Weight	Reps

MIND-BODY NOTES

NUTRITION NOTES

PLAYLIST

Cardio Activity:	
Average Heart Rate:	
Distance:	
Start Time:	End Time:

Date _____ Start Time _____ End Time _____

Type of set (Rest ____)	Exercise (Sets ____ × Reps ____)	Set 1		Set 2		Set 3		Set 4	
		Weight	Reps	Weight	Reps	Weight	Reps	Weight	Reps

MIND-BODY NOTES **NUTRITION NOTES** **PLAYLIST**

Cardio Activity:	
Average Heart Rate:	
Distance:	
Start Time:	End Time:

Date _____   Start Time _____   End Time _____

Type of set (Rest _____)	Exercise (Sets _____ × Reps _____)	Set 1		Set 2		Set 3		Set 4	
		Weight	Reps	Weight	Reps	Weight	Reps	Weight	Reps

MIND-BODY NOTES

NUTRITION NOTES

PLAYLIST

Cardio Activity:	
Average Heart Rate:	
Distance:	
Start Time:	End Time:

Date _____   Start Time _____   End Time _____

Type of set (Rest ____)	Exercise (Sets ____ × Reps ____)	Set 1		Set 2		Set 3		Set 4	
		Weight	Reps	Weight	Reps	Weight	Reps	Weight	Reps

MIND-BODY NOTES   **NUTRITION NOTES**   **PLAYLIST**

Cardio Activity:	
Average Heart Rate:	
Distance:	
Start Time:	End Time:

Date _____   Start Time _____   End Time _____

Type of set (Rest _____)	Exercise (Sets _____ × Reps _____)	Set 1 Weight	Reps	Set 2 Weight	Reps	Set 3 Weight	Reps	Set 4 Weight	Reps

MIND-BODY NOTES   **NUTRITION NOTES**   **PLAYLIST**

Cardio Activity:	
Average Heart Rate:	
Distance:	
Start Time:		End Time:	

Date _____ Start Time _____ End Time _____

Type of set (Rest ___)	Exercise (Sets ___ × Reps ___)	Set 1		Set 2		Set 3		Set 4	
		Weight	Reps	Weight	Reps	Weight	Reps	Weight	Reps

MIND-BODY NOTES

NUTRITION NOTES

PLAYLIST

Cardio Activity:	
Average Heart Rate:	
Distance:	
Start Time:	End Time:

Date _____   Start Time _____   End Time _____

Type of set (Rest ____)	Exercise (Sets ____ × Reps ____)	Set 1		Set 2		Set 3		Set 4	
		Weight	Reps	Weight	Reps	Weight	Reps	Weight	Reps

MIND-BODY NOTES	NUTRITION NOTES	PLAYLIST

Cardio Activity:	
Average Heart Rate:	
Distance:	
Start Time:	End Time:

Date _____   Start Time _____   End Time _____

Type of set (Rest _____)	Exercise (Sets _____ × Reps _____)	Set 1		Set 2		Set 3		Set 4	
		Weight	Reps	Weight	Reps	Weight	Reps	Weight	Reps

MIND-BODY NOTES	NUTRITION NOTES	PLAYLIST

Cardio Activity:	
Average Heart Rate:	
Distance:	
Start Time:	End Time:

Date _____   Start Time _____   End Time _____

Type of set (Rest ____)	Exercise (Sets ____ × Reps ____)	Set 1		Set 2		Set 3		Set 4	
		Weight	Reps	Weight	Reps	Weight	Reps	Weight	Reps

MIND-BODY NOTES

NUTRITION NOTES

PLAYLIST

Cardio Activity:	
Average Heart Rate:	
Distance:	
Start Time:	End Time:

Date _____ Start Time _____ End Time _____

Type of set (Rest ____)	Exercise (Sets ____ × Reps ____)	Set 1 Weight	Reps	Set 2 Weight	Reps	Set 3 Weight	Reps	Set 4 Weight	Reps

MIND-BODY NOTES **NUTRITION NOTES** **PLAYLIST**

Cardio Activity:	
Average Heart Rate:	
Distance:	
Start Time:	End Time:

Date _____   Start Time _____   End Time _____

Type of set (Rest ____)	Exercise (Sets ____ × Reps ____)	Set 1 Weight	Set 1 Reps	Set 2 Weight	Set 2 Reps	Set 3 Weight	Set 3 Reps	Set 4 Weight	Set 4 Reps

MIND-BODY NOTES

NUTRITION NOTES

PLAYLIST

Cardio Activity:	
Average Heart Rate:	
Distance:	
Start Time:	End Time:

Date _____   Start Time _____   End Time _____

Type of set (Rest _____)	Exercise (Sets _____ × Reps _____)	Set 1 Weight	Set 1 Reps	Set 2 Weight	Set 2 Reps	Set 3 Weight	Set 3 Reps	Set 4 Weight	Set 4 Reps

MIND-BODY NOTES

NUTRITION NOTES

PLAYLIST

Cardio Activity:	
Average Heart Rate:	
Distance:	
Start Time:	End Time:

Date _____   Start Time _____   End Time _____

Type of set (Rest ____)	Exercise (Sets ____ × Reps ____)	Set 1		Set 2		Set 3		Set 4	
		Weight	Reps	Weight	Reps	Weight	Reps	Weight	Reps

MIND-BODY NOTES

NUTRITION NOTES

PLAYLIST

Cardio Activity:	
Average Heart Rate:	
Distance:	
Start Time:	End Time:

Date _____ Start Time _____ End Time _____

Type of set (Rest _____)	Exercise (Sets _____ × Reps _____)	Set 1		Set 2		Set 3		Set 4	
		Weight	Reps	Weight	Reps	Weight	Reps	Weight	Reps

MIND-BODY NOTES

NUTRITION NOTES

PLAYLIST

Cardio Activity:	
Average Heart Rate:	
Distance:	
Start Time:		End Time:	

Date _____   Start Time _____   End Time _____

Type of set (Rest _____)	Exercise (Sets _____ × Reps _____)	Set 1		Set 2		Set 3		Set 4	
		Weight	Reps	Weight	Reps	Weight	Reps	Weight	Reps

MIND-BODY NOTES

NUTRITION NOTES

PLAYLIST

Cardio Activity:	
Average Heart Rate:	
Distance:	
Start Time:	End Time:

Date _____ Start Time _____ End Time _____

Type of set (Rest ____)	Exercise (Sets ____ × Reps ____)	Set 1		Set 2		Set 3		Set 4	
		Weight	Reps	Weight	Reps	Weight	Reps	Weight	Reps

MIND-BODY NOTES

NUTRITION NOTES

PLAYLIST

Cardio Activity:	
Average Heart Rate:	
Distance:	
Start Time:	End Time:

Date _____   Start Time _____   End Time _____

Type of set (Rest _____)	Exercise (Sets _____ × Reps _____)	Set 1		Set 2		Set 3		Set 4	
		Weight	Reps	Weight	Reps	Weight	Reps	Weight	Reps

MIND-BODY NOTES   **NUTRITION NOTES**   **PLAYLIST**

Cardio Activity:	
Average Heart Rate:	
Distance:	
Start Time:	End Time:

Date _____   Start Time _____   End Time _____

Type of set (Rest ____)	Exercise (Sets ____ × Reps ____)	Set 1		Set 2		Set 3		Set 4	
		Weight	Reps	Weight	Reps	Weight	Reps	Weight	Reps

MIND-BODY NOTES   **NUTRITION NOTES**   **PLAYLIST**

Cardio Activity:	
Average Heart Rate:	
Distance:	
Start Time:	End Time:

Date _____   Start Time _____   End Time _____

Type of set (Rest ____)	Exercise (Sets ____ × Reps ____)	Set 1		Set 2		Set 3		Set 4	
		Weight	Reps	Weight	Reps	Weight	Reps	Weight	Reps

MIND-BODY NOTES	NUTRITION NOTES	PLAYLIST

Cardio Activity:	
Average Heart Rate:	
Distance:	
Start Time:	End Time:

Date _____   Start Time _____   End Time _____

Type of set (Rest ____)	Exercise (Sets ____ × Reps ____)	Set 1		Set 2		Set 3		Set 4	
		Weight	Reps	Weight	Reps	Weight	Reps	Weight	Reps

MIND-BODY NOTES   **NUTRITION NOTES**   **PLAYLIST**

Cardio Activity:	
Average Heart Rate:	
Distance:	
Start Time:	End Time:

Date _____   Start Time _____   End Time _____

Type of set (Rest ___)	Exercise (Sets ___ × Reps ___)	Set 1		Set 2		Set 3		Set 4	
		Weight	Reps	Weight	Reps	Weight	Reps	Weight	Reps

MIND-BODY NOTES   **NUTRITION NOTES**   **PLAYLIST**

Cardio Activity:	
Average Heart Rate:	
Distance:	
Start Time:	End Time:

Date _____   Start Time _____   End Time _____

Type of set (Rest ____)	Exercise (Sets ____ × Reps ____)	Set 1		Set 2		Set 3		Set 4	
		Weight	Reps	Weight	Reps	Weight	Reps	Weight	Reps

MIND-BODY NOTES   **NUTRITION NOTES**   **PLAYLIST**

Cardio Activity:	
Average Heart Rate:	
Distance:	
Start Time:	End Time:

Date _____   Start Time _____   End Time _____

Type of set (Rest _____)	Exercise (Sets _____ × Reps _____)	Set 1		Set 2		Set 3		Set 4	
		Weight	Reps	Weight	Reps	Weight	Reps	Weight	Reps

MIND-BODY NOTES	NUTRITION NOTES	PLAYLIST

Cardio Activity:	
Average Heart Rate:	
Distance:	

Start Time:		End Time:	

Date _____   Start Time _____   End Time _____

Type of set (Rest ____)	Exercise (Sets ____ × Reps ____)	Set 1 Weight	Reps	Set 2 Weight	Reps	Set 3 Weight	Reps	Set 4 Weight	Reps

MIND-BODY NOTES	NUTRITION NOTES	PLAYLIST

Cardio Activity:	
Average Heart Rate:	
Distance:	
Start Time:	End Time:

Date _____ Start Time _____ End Time _____

Type of set (Rest ____)	Exercise (Sets ____ × Reps ____)	Set 1		Set 2		Set 3		Set 4	
		Weight	Reps	Weight	Reps	Weight	Reps	Weight	Reps

MIND-BODY NOTES   **NUTRITION NOTES**   **PLAYLIST**

Cardio Activity:	
Average Heart Rate:	
Distance:	
Start Time:	End Time:

Date _____ Start Time _____ End Time _____

Type of set (Rest _____)	Exercise (Sets _____ × Reps _____)	Set 1 Weight	Set 1 Reps	Set 2 Weight	Set 2 Reps	Set 3 Weight	Set 3 Reps	Set 4 Weight	Set 4 Reps

MIND-BODY NOTES

NUTRITION NOTES

PLAYLIST

Cardio Activity:	
Average Heart Rate:	
Distance:	
Start Time:	End Time: